ANIMALS

LOOKING AT

Chris Dunn

Hodder & Stoughton
A MEMBER OF THE HODDER HEADLINE GROUP

Introduction: animals

Antonio Pisano, called Pisanello (1395–1455/6), **A dromedary,** pen and faint brown ink, 29.2 x 42.3 cm (11⅜ x 16½ inches), Royal Collection Enterprises.

The drawing of a dromedary by the Italian artist Pisanello is descriptive. The animal is being held so still that every detail can be captured. It is a curiosity, and it could be asleep or stuffed for all the life it shows.

This book includes illustrations of works of art and craft from different cultures. Each culture has its own set of values. These values satisfy the taste and style of that culture at a particular period of history. It is not surprising that we sometimes find them hard to understand. If you are eager enough to want to understand them, you must look at them in context, and try not to judge them by your own values.

Activity

Look at the drawings on these pages. You will see they come from different places with quite different traditions.

Make a survey of the illustrations in this book.

Can you discover what the artists intended for their work? Was it to be descriptive, imaginative or decorative?

Create a list of the illustrations from each category that you can find. Are there any illustrations that you cannot place?

Evaluation

Share your list with others in your group. Remember these are your ideas, there is no right or wrong answer.

Discuss your ideas and resolve any disagreements.

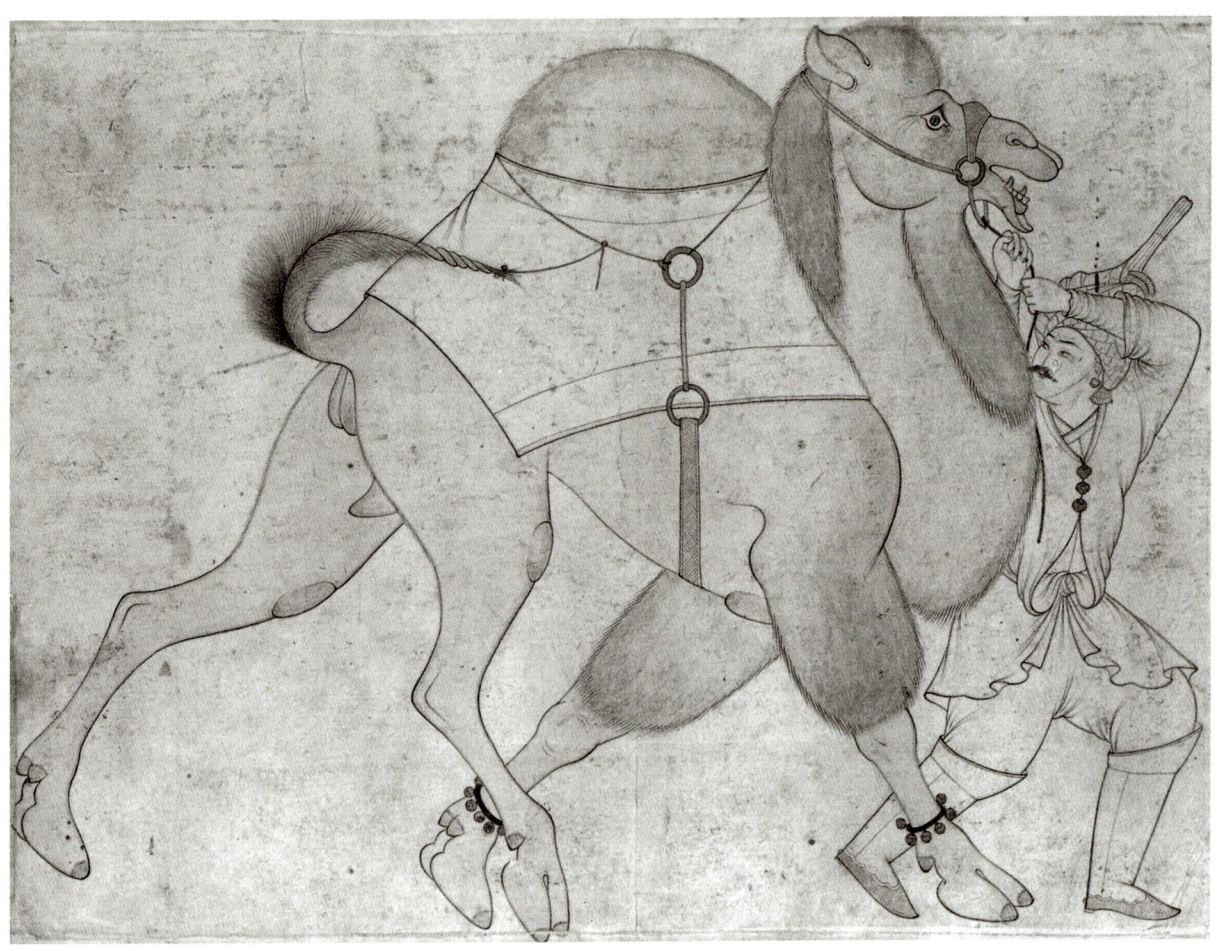

Owned by Shakyh Muhammed, **Man and camel**, c.1545, drawing using ink, gold and colour on paper, 28.5 x 40.6 cm (11⅛ x 15¹³⁄₁₆ inches), Cleveland Museum of Art, Ohio.

This Iranian camel contrasts with the dromedary on the opposite page. It looks very much alive and quite a handful for the groom. It is full of vitality and movement. The variety in thickness and weight of the line the artist uses makes the camel almost flicker across the page.

Extension

Find examples of animal pictures that appear in their different cultures. Make a list of the works that you have found. Write the identities clearly.

Note the cultures and the period that each work comes from. Mark them on a world map and on a timeline.

Computer option

Enter simple facts about these works of art in a database. What categories can you find to group the works?

The artist's name (alphabetical), dates, types of material used, sizes and where they can now be found are all important details. This information is usually available in the caption to each piece of work.

3

Animals as symbols

Jan Gosseart (active 1503, died 1532),
The Adoration of the Kings, 1508–9,
oil on oak panel, 177.2 x 161.3 cm (69 1/16 x 23 7/8 inches),
The National Gallery, London.

Sometimes artists put images in their work which have extra or symbolic meaning. Animals can be particularly expressive. The artist has included a dog in this painting for a reason. It is used as a symbol of faithfulness.

Activity

Make a list of the animals used in other paintings. Write down what they stand for and the details of the work you found them in.

Create a picture of your own, a self portrait, or a portrait of a friend. Use some animals to give extra meaning to your picture.

Jan Gosseart (active 1503; died 1532),
Detail taken from **The Adoration of the Kings**, 1508–9,
oil on oak panel,
177.2 x 161.3 cm (69 1/16 x 23 7/8 inches),
The National Gallery, London.

Discussion points

★ Has the use of symbols changed since the time this painting was done?

★ Think of new symbols you might use in your work.

Evaluation

Mount an exhibition that shows your research into symbols. Show how you have used symbols in your own work. Invite the comments of your friends.

Do they agree with the way you have used the symbols? Could they suggest better ones that have come from their research? Can you see ways in which your image could have developed further?

Write a commentary on your own work.

Extension

Symbols are often used in advertising to give products more interest and appeal to the consumer. Tigers make petrol more exciting, penguins make chocolate biscuits more exotic. Ordinary products like pans or children's toys become high-flying eagles or reliable oak trees. Look for as many examples as you can find, and comment upon the most and least suitable use of symbols.

The importance of captions

Activity

Cover up the caption of the picture. Examine the picture closely. How much information can you get just from looking at it?

Now, uncover the caption and answer the questions.

1. Who painted the picture?
2. When was the artist alive, and when was the picture painted?
3. What it its title?
4. What materials were used to create it?
5. Where can it be seen today?
6. What is its size? (Remember, the height is always given first.)

Is the information in the caption useful or can it be ignored?

Write your answers in full sentences.

Do some research of your own to find out more about the painting.

Jan van Eyck (active 1422, died 1441), **The portrait of Gianovanni (?) Arnolfini and his wife Giovanna Cenami (?) 'The Arnolfini Marriage'**, 1434, oil on oak, 81.8 x 59.7 cm (31⅞ x 23⅜ inches), The National Gallery, London.

Discussion point

★ This painting has been studied by many scholars. Different interpretations have been given to all the symbolic images in the painting. What features of the painting do you think have extra meaning?

In case you think that only dogs are faithful to humans, this example shows the reverse can also be true. This casket is the last resting place of what was obviously a much loved and valued pet. It was made of Tunbridge Well Ware, a form of marquetry using inlays of different wood types, in 1883. The dog has been preserved by a taxidermist. It is a Chinese Lu-lu terrier. The casket, which would have been kept in the owner's home, was built like a shrine.

Activity

From the information given write a detailed caption for the work on this page.

Evaluation

Compare your answers with those of a friend. Which of you has the most convincing caption to the dog's casket?

George Stubbs – animal artist

George Stubbs (1724–1806), **Mares and Foals in a Landscape**, c.1763–68, oil on canvas, 102 x 162 cm (39⅝ x 36⁷⁄₁₆ inches), Tate Gallery, London.

George Stubbs was one of the foremost animal artists of the 18th century. Before Stubbs, animal painting was one of the least-regarded areas for an up-and-coming artist to work in. Stubbs took his work very seriously. He studied anatomy in order to better represent the horses. At one time he had a dead horse hanging in his studio so that he could examine its anatomy as it decomposed!

Activity

1. Can you write a simple definition of all the words in the word bank? Use a dictionary to help you.

   Explain how these words might help you when studying art.

2. Look at one of the pieces of work on these pages.

   Write a short article for a magazine about one of these pictures. Use the caption to the picture as a starting point, but add your own ideas too. The words in the word bank will help focus your thoughts.

Word bank

space   mood   detail   colour
depth   line   movement   reflection
texture   pattern   direction   volume
distance   atmosphere   materials   function
light   security   character   vitality
subject   media   exotic   design

3. Create a modern setting for the background to 'Mares and Foals in a Landscape' or 'Whistlejacket'.

George Stubbs (1724–1806), **Whistlejacket,**
1762, oil on canvas,
292 x 246.4 cm (113⅞ x 96 inches),
The National Gallery, London.

Computer option

Research

Use the information on a CD-ROM, or use the Internet, to research the artist George Stubbs. Find out all you can about him and his paintings. If you print all the information you find, you will probably get far more than you need. Read the print-outs and edit them so that you have a selection of the most useful pieces of information.

Remember

Decide what you need to know. Use a highlighter to pick out the information.
Rewrite the highlighted sections.
Always check through to make sure you understand what you have written
Word process and spell check your work. Remember to say where your information came from.

Extension

Use the research plan to write about the work of another artist whose work you like. You could look at the artist whose work is in this book. Make an illustrated presentation of your research. Use the word bank on p8 to help you get started.

Bestiaries

Illustrations from **The Pepysian Sketchbook**, 14th century, drawing on parchment, 24.8 x 18.2 cm (9^{11}/$_{16}$ x 7^{1}/$_{8}$ inches), Pepysian Library, Magdelene College, Cambridge.

These pages are from a rare catalogue of designs collected over many years, generations even, by medieval artists. Customers could choose the designs they liked to decorate their church or castle.

Travellers have often written about meeting or seeing strange animals. Frequently their descriptions are far more dramatic than the truth. To travellers in ancient times, like the Greeks and Romans, the natural world was full of the unexplained.

European travellers and explorers were just as willing to believe that there were creatures even more marvellous than the elephant, giraffe or hippopotamus. They sent back stories of giant crocodiles and tribes of gorillas living a life of 'civilisation' deep in the jungle. Mythical and real creatures were often recorded and described together in books called **bestiaries**.

Activity

Can you find out about unusual or mythical creatures? What are the tales behind the Sphinx, the Phoenix and the Cyclops?

Activity

Design a double page spread for a bestiary. Create some creatures of your own, but include some real animals too. If each person in the class creates a page of description and an illustration, then the whole set can be put together to form a class bestiary.

Look at some real, perhaps domestic, animals and make some sketches. If you cannot find any real animals, look at illustrations in books or on CD-ROM. For each new creature you will need to think of a name, a description and some information on where it lives and how.

William de Morgan (1839–1917),
Tile designs, 1870s–1880s, 15.2 cm (6 inch) square,
lustre tiles in pencil and watercolour,
Victoria & Albert Museum, London.

Evaluation

As your work will be bound and displayed with the work of others in your group, you must make sure you contribution maintains its quality.

Perhaps your could consider publishing a copy of the finished bestiary for distribution to family and friends.

Extension

An introduction and a cover for the book will also be required. If you finish your individual work you might like to try to create one or the other.

Bird study

Albrecht Durer (1471–1528),
Study of the wing of a European Roller, 1524,
watercolour and pencil,
18.9 x 23.8 cm (7⁵/₁₆ x 9⁵/₁₆ inches),
Christies, London.

Durer was inspired by the feather-work being brought back from Mexico and the other New World territories controlled by Spain. Many new tropical plant and animal species where first seen in this way.

Activity

Find some feathers of your own and make studies in your sketchbook. Even the feathers of common birds can be of interest.

A *study sheet* is a way of putting all the information about a subject in one place. Make a study sheet based on the theme of feathers. You could collect some examples from different birds, make sketches, prints, photograms or rubbings of them. You might like to find out how wings work and make written notes.

Can you find out about man's early attempts to fly using feathers?

Not only did Howard Carter see the Hoopoe nesting under the painted wings of the vulture goddess Nekubet, he also saw a chance to comment on the durability of nature, as opposed to the works of man. How do you think he manages this?

Evaluation

Make an exhibition of drawn study sheets in your class. Examine the finished pieces of work and choose one that you all agree is best. On your own decide why you like it and then compare your reasons.

Do you all agree?

Howard Carter (1837–1939),
Hoopoe nesting under the wings of the vulture goddess Nekhubet, 1922, watercolour, 65.4 x 47.4 cm (25½ x 18½ inches), (British Museum), private colletion, London.

Extension

Through your bird studies try and develop a methodical use of your sketchbook.

A sketch is a drawing that helps you to understand your subject. It can help you plan ahead, and give you information. Sometimes written notes, or annotations, are an important part of a sketch.

You might want to use some colour over part of the sketch.

You might only make one visit to a site. It is important to get as much information as possible while you are there.

How will your sketches be used? If you want to make descriptive pictures, for example, you will need factual information, even measurement details. It might help if you write your intentions before sketching, to help focus your mind.

Above all, you must use your curiosity. It will lead you round the next corner and to the solutions and unresolved problems that fill every good artist's sketchbook.

Looking at peacocks

This is a lifesize model of a peacock. It can be found in the Minton museum in Stoke-on-Trent. Another copy can be found in the Flagstaff Hill Memorial Village Warrnabool, Australia. It survived a shipwreck and was washed ashore where it was rescued.

Paul Comolera (designer) (1818–1897), **Peacock**, 1873, lifesize, 153 cm (60 inches), earthenware (clay), Minton Museum, Stoke-on-Trent.

Activity

Make some study drawings of a live peacock. See if you can get a peacock's tail-feather, or pictures that show the whole tail display, it may help you.

Collect other images of decorative birds. Be selective as there are a lot! If you have access to a CD-ROM look up John James Audubon's 'Birds of America'.

Create, in any medium you like, a decorative bird or series of birds. From them produce a finished piece.

It may be a brightly patterned piece of work, perhaps in fabric crayons on material.

Can you translate your designs to a 3D image?

Exotic birds often appear in paintings. Some Dutch paintings of the 17th century show the importance of Holland's trade routes. Many of the fabulous creatures found along the 'spice routes' to Indonesia were unknown back in Holland. The artists took great care to make their pictures accurate. The paintings were the only way discoveries could be shared. Since the 17th century many species of animals and birds have disappeared and the only record of what they looked like is to be found in these works.

René Lalique (1860–1945), **Decorative peacock lamp**, c. 1925, moulded and etched glass, 45 cm high (17⅝ inches), Victoria & Albert Museum, London.

Discussion point

René Lalique was a French designer who produced an amazing variety of beautiful objects, both decorative and practical, out of glass. His work is still sought after today. What other information can you find out about him?

Extension

Find some examples of extinct species that can be seen in paintings. Try and draw from them. Alternatively, visit a museum and examine the birds on display there.

Evaluation

Discuss with your friends the birds you have created.

Are they believable?

In what other ways could they have been presented ?

You might like to group the birds you have created by their characteristics, for example, 'patterned feathers' or 'interesting shapes'.

15

Studying cats

Thomas Gainsborough (1722–1788), **Six studies of a cat,** 1763–69, pencil, highlighted with white chalk on brown paper, 33.2 x 45.9 cm (12⅞ x 17⅞ inches), Rijksmuseum, Amsterdam.

Over 20% of all households in Britain have cats. Perhaps you have one at home, if not find someone who has and will let you draw it. Before you draw the cat, you should be prepared to watch it carefully. It may be the nearest you will get to a really wild animal.

Thomas Gainsborough completed these cat sketches on the same day. Highlighting a sketch with white chalk may be a technique you would like to try in your work.

Activity

Even a cat at rest can show glimpses of the wild animal inside. The artists whose work is on these pages clearly knew their cats well.

Make a study sheet using the detailed knowledge you have gained from cat-watching.

Make drawings in your sketchbook, then use these drawings in your study work.

Collect written descriptions and poetry about cats. Your study sheet should be selective showing only what you think is important about your cat. Try and decide what makes your chosen cat an individual.

Create a mask, or series of masks that show your cat as an individual character.

You might like to experiment with ways of moving like a cat to bring your masks to life. The musical 'Cats' shows how this can be done.

Attributed to Katsukawa Shunso (1726–1792),
Cat licking its paw, c.1789–92, hanging scroll on paper,
38 x 51 cm (14 13/16 x 19 15/16 inches),
British Museum, London.

The artists on these pages view their cats very differently. Thomas Gainsborough and Katsukawa Shunso were working about the same time. What influences make their cats so different?

Evaluation

Discuss with your group how individual you have made your mask.

Can they see things in your cat character that you have missed?

Activity

Create a netsuke of your own. Usually netsuke were carved from ivory, but you can make one from clay. They were hollow, and were used as toggle for a cord belt. It should be small and light. Use your knowledge of cats to create an original piece of your own.

Tomin (signed), 18th century,
Japanese netsuke, or ornamental toggle,
made from wood inlaid with mother of pearl,
Victoria & Albert Museum, London.

Tigers

By concentrating on the pattern elements of the tiger's striped coat, and the ferocity of its gaze, the artist has created a fearful beast. Tigers could still be found in Japan at the time this scroll was painted.

Drawing from observation is an important part of your course. It is essential that you draw from 'life', that is with real objects in front of you. Sometimes, however, this is not possible.

Kishi Ganky (1749-1838), **Tiger** c.1784–96, ink-painted silk scroll hangings, 169 x 114.5 cm (65⅞ x 44⅝ inches), British Museum, London.

Activity

Find out more about tigers. Use information from books, pictures, stories, and poems. Create a study sheet. Make drawings for your collection, but be sure not to copy. Try exaggerating physical aspects of the animal to reveal its character.

Concentrate on the striped pattern of the coat. Change the colours used and the frequency of the stripes. What make the best camouflage for the animal?

Concentrate on the teeth of the tiger. How can you make a more aggressive looking beast?

Show the spirit of the animal and not just its outwards appearance.

Develop from your study a creative and original piece of work to express your feelings for this animal.

Henri Rousseau (1844–1910),
Tiger in a tropical storm (surprised!), 1891,
oil on canvas,
129.8 x 161.9 cm (50⅝ x 63¾₆ inches), The National Gallery, London.

Rousseau worked as a customs officer on the Belgian border, and apart from a short spell as a soldier on garrison duty in France, he rarely left the small part of France where he worked. He had never seen a tiger and painted using his imagination, black and white newspaper cuttings and the descriptions printed in books. Yet he was still able to convey the spirit of the tiger, terrified by a storm, rushing through its jungle home.

Discussion points

★ Can you find artists whose work includes tigers drawn from life?

★ Look at the ways these two artists have solved the problem of drawing from life.

Evaluation

Mount an exhibition of your study sheets and the creative work that has developed from them. Discuss the work with others in your group.

Can you identify, in agreement with others, three things that you need to do to improve your work?

Make a note of these points on the reverse of your study sheet. Include anything you have thought of as well.

Write a short critical study of your work using the notes you have made.

Lions

**Assyrian lion,
relief carved in stone,**
645BC, 106 x 124 cm (41⅜ x 48⅜ inches),
British Museum, London.

The Assyrian lion was about the size of a St Bernard dog. It is now extinct. At the time it was alive, the only person allowed to kill one in the Assyrian Empire was the King. This panel represents the death of a lion as it tries to fight back. This method of recording the most dramatic kills was common in Assyria.

We're fascinated by the ferocious beasts that once preyed on our ancestors. Whenever we visit them in a zoo, it is easy to imagine what might happen if they escaped.

Discussion point

★ Can you remember seeing real lions? Describe your impressions.

Activity

The lion is an animal that is often used in heraldry. It can be seen on the Queen's standard and on the England football shirt. When it is standing on its hind legs it is said to be 'rampant'. You can also find it on the back of the ten-pence coin.

Make a study sheet to show the many uses of this heraldic lion. If it has been used as a trademark you might like to collect examples of it in use.

From your study sheet and using all the information you collect, design a heraldic lion of your own. Perhaps it could be for a badge for a sport shirt. Your study sheet will provide you with the knowledge and confidence to tackle this difficult task.

Dying Lioness c.645 BC, detail from the Palace Ashurbanipal, Nineveh, carving, low stone relief, British Museum, London.

Extension

Research

Study sheets show how well you have researched your project. They can contain drawings, colour or tonal studies, as well as factual information. They may contain copies of pictures that you have found inspirational, perhaps poetry or the written word.

They can provide essential backup for your final piece, showing the development route to your final work.

Make your study sheets as interesting as possible, they help show how much the subject interested you.

Even when pierced with so many arrows this dying lioness drags herself towards her tormentors. What does this tell you about the artist's feeling about the lioness?

Evaluation

Make a presentation that shows the development of your particular symbol. Take it in turns to present your version of the task to the whole group. Explain why you have taken the decisions about size, shape, form and colour that you have.

Elephants

Rembrandt van Rijn (1606–1669), **Elephant**, drawn from life, 1634, black chalk, 17.8 x 25.6 cm (6⅞ x 9⅞ inches), British Museum, London.

Any description of an elephant to someone who has never seen or heard of such a creature sounds unreal. When elephants first came to 17th century Holland they were a curiosity, an oddity to be studied. Contrast Rembrandt's approach to his subject with Pisanello's approach (see page 2). Both treat the animal as a still life subject, a specimen to be drawn. In both cases there is not much 'life'.

Contrast this drawing with other work from countries where elephants were an everyday part of the landscape, such as India.

Discussion point

★ If you had never seen an elephant, would you be able to describe one?

Moghul painting on the façade of a merchant haveli of a Raja on an elephant, Rajasthan, India, c.1850–60, pigment on pure lime plaster, around 184 cm high, (72 inches), Images of India Picture Agency.

Activity

Make a study sheet on the theme of elephants. From your study sheet create a brief description of no more than 40 words that describe the elephant's most important characteristics. Pass your description on to a friend and collect one from them.

Draw only what the description tells you. What sort of animal do you create? It will no doubt be elephant-like.

Extend this piece of work by making a set of animal cards, each with a different animal on it. Follow the same process as before, this time trying to guess what the animal is using drawn interpretations of the writer's description.

Use the word bank to help you with the written description of an elephant.

Word bank

trunk   skin   ears   size   legs   length   colour   firm   number
texture   movement   feel   shape   volume   feel   touch

Evaluation

Make a presentation of your study sheets and the written descriptions. Try to match the illustration with the written description it was drawn from.

23

Strange creatures

We like to see live animals which is why wildlife parks and zoos are still so popular. We know from books and from documentaries on television what most animals look like, yet this is only a shadow of the real thing.

Discussion point

★ Imagine you were seeing a creature for the first time. What points would you be looking for?

Moriz Jung, **Giraffe**, c. early 20th century.

Activity

Find some animals that are very unusual, that you haven't seen before. What, for example does an Aardwolf look like?

Use the animal's name to write a brief description of it. Pass your description to another member of the class and ask them to draw the animal.

Do not use comparisons in your description. Do not, for example, say an animal is striped like a zebra. Imagine you know nothing of wild animals' shapes and colours.

Mansur Moghal, **A Zebra**, 1621,
gouche on paper,
24 x 18.3 cm (9⁹⁄₁₆ x 7⅛ inches),
Victoria & Albert Museum, London.

Do you know that a camelopard is? or what a liger or tigron might be?

The camelopard was the name originally given to the giraffe. The liger and tigron are names given to animals that resulted from the breeding of lions and tigers.

Did you know that the story of the horn of the unicorn developed from examples of the extended tooth of the male narwhal? Strange creatures were often created in people's imagination and drawn or described for fun.

This painting was completed in order to record what the zebra looked like and is a good representation.

Activity

Make a drawn record of some of the strangest creatures you can find out about.

Evaluation

How good is your version of the animal when compared to the written description?

Does it match the description?

Make an exhibition of pictures. Mix up the descriptions, can you link the correct description to each animal?

Anthropomorphism

George Turner (b.1961), collection of illustrations from portfolio, (1999), courtesy of George Turner.

Combining animals and human shapes or giving animals human characteristics is a favourite method of cartoonists and advertisers. This is known as **anthropomorphism**. We are so used to it that we rarely take any notice of the unreal situation of say, a mouse talking in a cartoon, or a real dragon advertising breakfast cereal. In the illustrations on this page, George Turner has managed to make the gorilla dumb but likable, the snail scholarly and the crocodile into a street-wise heavy.

Can you find examples, perhaps from children's books or advertisements, where animals have been given human characteristics?

Activity

Based on some careful drawings from observation, create a character of your own. In groups agree what characteristics each of you will portray. Use the list to help you.

Word bank

silly shy mean heroic
sly victim unlucky wise

Can you think of a cartoon character that fits each description?

Imagine you are trying to persuade a television company to make a children's film with your character in it. Make a presentation of your character.

Alan Baker (b.1951),
Cockerel head on a human body,
(1997), illustration, pen and ink,
watercolour and airbrush, courtesy of
Alan Baker.

Anon, **Ganesh** c.12th–13th century,
carved from chloritic schist,
85 cm high (33³⁄₁₆ inches),
Werner Forman Archive.

The illustration of the cockerel's head is a little sinister. It could be a mask, but it does seem to fit rather well – perhaps it is real!

The Indian god Ganesh is a symbol of good luck. School children in India often have a picture printed onto the front cover of their exercise books. The god has the head of an elephant but the body, though blessed with an extra set of arms, is human.

Evaluation

Create an animal mask, the technique you use is for you to decide. It could be a simple card shape, or a more complex papier mâché head formed around a balloon. Make your mask as real as possible. Look how successful the cockerel is. Photograph your finished mask.

27

Studying the horse

Horse of Selene, from the East pediment of the Parthenon, Athens c. 438–432 BC, marble, 79 cm in length (30 13/16 inches), British Museum, London.

Horses have been admired for generations for their many qualities. They have inspired many artists. This sculpture forms part of the collection made by Lord Elgin in the 19th century. The Horse of Selene was one of the horses used by the moon goddess (Selene) to pull the moon around the sky.

For a very long time even the most accomplished artists did not really understand their subject. The way a horse moved, in particular at a gallop, was a mystery and caused endless argument. Most artists imagined that the horses legs moved in pairs. They thought that at a certain point in a gallop all the horses legs were off the ground.

Activity

Create a piece of work that describes one aspect of the horse's character that you most admire. Is it the speed, strength, endurance, or its grace and beauty? Try to choose a medium which is in sympathy with the characteristics you have chosen to highlight.

Look at the work of the other artists whose work you admire. You might for example choose the French artist Theodore Gericault whose drawing on page 29 shows the power and grace of the charging beast.

Theodore Gericault (1791–1824), **Rearing horse**, 1812, drawing, Louvre, RMN, Paris.

Even artists like George Stubbs found it hard to understand the horses' movements and he was considered an expert on the anatomy of the horse. The name of this imagined movement was the 'flying gallop'. It seems to express the vigour and speed of the way a horse moved at speed. The problem was, horses never move like this.

In 1878 a man called Edward Muybridge published a series of photographs of a horse passing a set of equally placed markers at a gallop. In the photographs he clearly showed how a horse moved at speed, and suddenly all the paintings of horses in motion looked dated and old fashioned.

Evaluation

Are you pleased with the way you have worked?

Discuss your work with a friend and see if you can share three things you are unhappy about. Write them down and then return to your work and try to put them right. If you can correct them repeat the process with a different friend.

Activity

Can you find examples of Muybridge's work?

Horse and man

Amber head, 17th century, gouche on paper, 23.4 x 30.3 cm (9⅛ x 11¹³⁄₁₆ inches), British Museum, London. This portrait of a horse forms part of an inventory of possessions of an Indian ruler.

The wonder of the horse and man's relationship to it is a theme which has been celebrated by artists through the centuries.

Evaluation

Make a written commentary of what you have found and list the qualities that you think have made your choice so successful. Compare your lists and discuss the qualities that all your artists have brought to the subject.

Activity

Create a study sheet based on your drawings of horses and in particular their heads. If you can, work from life, otherwise use all the secondary sources available to you.

Which of the illustrations on these pages do you think is taken from real life and which is worked from an already existing artist's work? Explain your reasoning.

As part of your study sheet make a study of the way different artists and different cultures have shown the horse throughout history. List your source material in some sort of systematic way and try to decide which artist or group have been most successful and why.

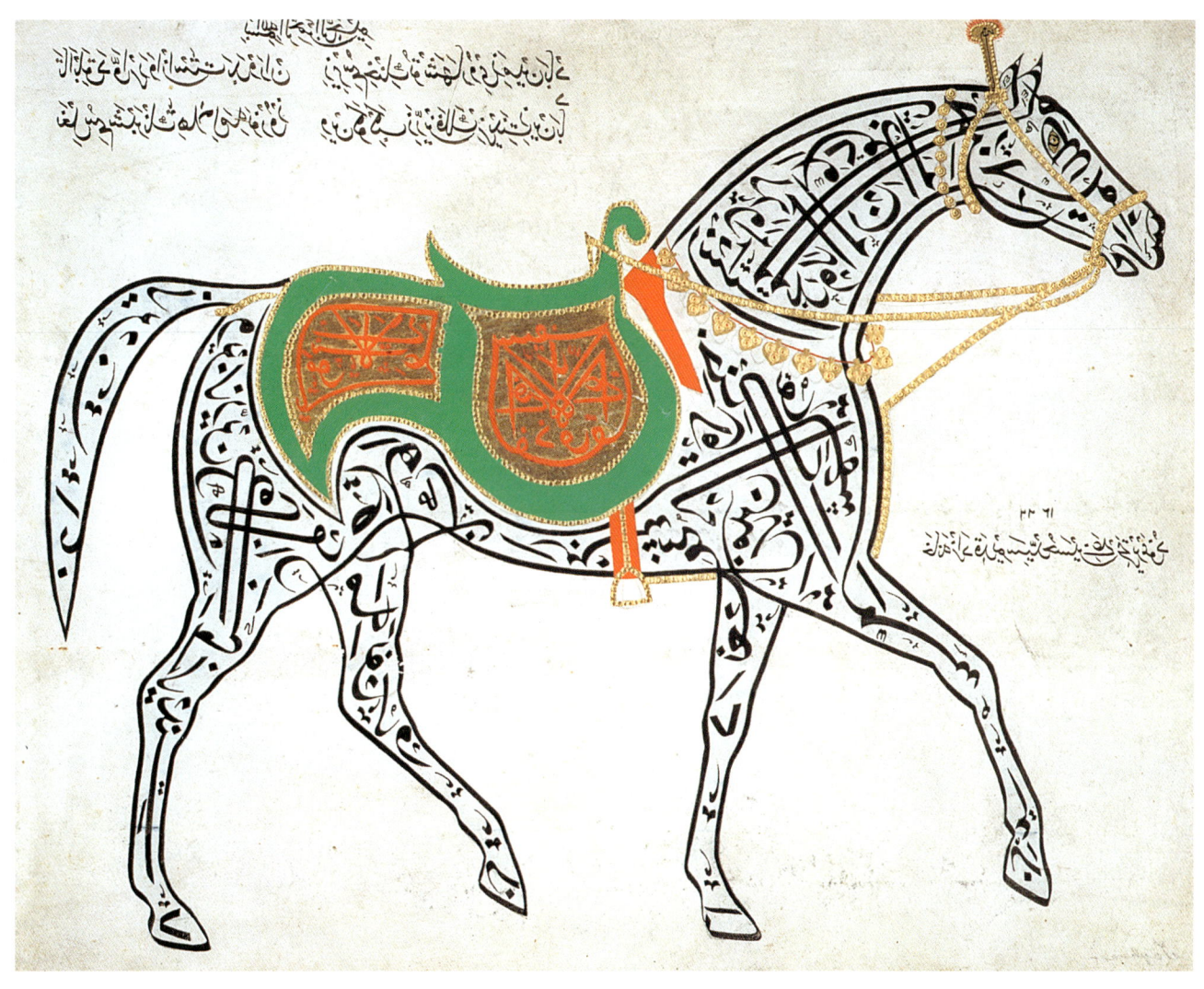

Iranian calligram in the form of a horse, in praise of a horse, 1849–50, 36.2 x 44.3 cm (14⅛ x 17⁷⁄₁₆ inches), Victoria & Albert Museum, London.

Extension

Research

Some artists have created a lot of work based on the images of the horse. Choose one of those named below and write a short illustrated account of their work.

Edgar Degas (1834–1917)

Marino Marini (1901–1980)

Eugene Delacroix (1798–1863)

Sir Alfred Munnings (1875–1959)

Theodore Gericault (1791–1824)

You do not need to write a great deal.

If you use illustrations you must be sure to caption them.

Write a short introduction.

Write a biography of the artist with dates.

Then write about any illustrations you have included.

Most importantly, write about your reaction to the work – if you like it say why, if you don't explain why not.

For Dianne, Serena, Beech and Sapphire

Acknowledgements

The publishers would like to thank the following individuals, institutions and companies for permission to reproduce photographs in this book. Every effort has been made to trace ownership of copyright. The publishers will be happy to make arrangements with any copyright holder whom it has not been possible to contact.

Alan Baker 27 (left); British Museum, London 17 (top), 18, 20, 21, 22, 28, 30; Christie's Images 12; Cleveland Museum of Art 3; George Turner 26; Images of India Picture agency 23; Magdalene College, Cambridge 10; Minton Museum, Stoke-on-Trent 14; Private Collection 13; Rijks Museum, Amsterdam 16; RMN Paris 29; Royal Collection Enterprises 2; The National Gallery, London 4, 5, 6, 9, 19; The Tate Gallery, London 8; Tunbridge Wells Museum 7; Victoria & Albert Museum 11, 15,17 (bottom), 25, 31; Werner Forman Archive 27 (right).

Orders: please contact Bookpoint Ltd, 78 Milton Park, Abingdon, Oxon OX14 4TD. Telephone: (44) 01235 827720, Fax: (44) 01235 400454. Lines are open from 9.00 - 6.00, Monday to Saturday, with a 24 hour message answering service. Email address: orders@bookpoint.co.uk

British Library Cataloguing in Publication Data
A catalogue record for this title is available from The British Library

ISBN 0 340 66417 7

First published 2000
Impression number 10 9 8 7 6 5 4 3 2 1
Year   2005 2004 2003 2002 2001 2000

Copyright © 2000 Chris Dunn

All rights reserved. No part of this publication may be reproduced or transmitted in any form or by any means, electronic or mechanical, including photocopy, recording, or any information storage and retrieval system, without permission in writing from the publisher or under licence from the Copyright Licensing Agency Limited. Further details of such licences (for reprographic reproduction) may be obtained from the Copyright Licensing Agency Limited, of 90 Tottenham Court Road, London W1P 9HE.

Cover photo Attributed to Katsukawa Shunso (1726–1792) **Cat licking its paw**, hanging scroll on paper, (380 x 510 mm), British Museum, London.
Designed by Lynda King
Typeset by Carla Turchini
Picture research by Suzanne O'Farrell
Printed in Dubai, U.A.E. for Hodder & Stoughton Educational, a division of Hodder Headline Plc, 338 Euston Road, London NW1 3BH by Oriental Press